Use these stickers for the activities in the book

Page 2

Page 4

b b b

Page 7

w w

w w

Page 8

ng ng

ng ng

Page 11

a a a

a a

Page 13

cl cl

gl gl

Pages 2–3

Here's a mouse!

Here's a mouse!

Here's a mouse!

Page 16

Why must you go?

I forgot the time!

Page 18

Page 20

Page 14

ere air ear are

Page 17

j j g g

Page 21

c k

Page 22

nd nd

nd nd

Page 24

Cinderella

near clap

wing glass

patch just

magic kind

Treat yourself to a gold star the

Well done!

Well done!

Well done!

Well done!

Well done!

Well done!

Well done!

Well done!

Well done!

Well done!

Get Set Go Phonics

Cinderella

Phonics Consultant: Susan Purcell

Illustrator: Giuliana Gregori

Concept: Fran Bromage

Miles Kelly

Read aloud focusing on the s sound (as in silly)

Once upon a time, there was a girl called Cinderella, who often felt sad.

She had two silly stepsisters, and a stepmother who was not very nice to her.

Use your arrow stickers to **point** to three mice.

Say the names as you spot each person.

Stick on their stickers.

2

Cinderella

 sister

sister

Cinderella worked hard, but the sisters were never satisfied. Every night Cinderella sat by the fireside with the mice.

What a good try! Put a gold star here.

Sound out these words with the s sound.

ice   saucer   set   sell

circus   city   ceiling

3

One day the two stepsisters were being beastly to Cinderella, when a letter arrived.

It was an invitation to a ball at the palace, but Cinderella's stepmother banned her from going.

Use your stickers to **spell** some words beginning with b.

bake   box   bear   bird   bulb

4

Instead, Cinderella had to help both her bossy sisters get ready for the ball.

"We look fabulous," they boasted.

Say the names of the things in the pictures as you find them. They all use the **b** sound.

bows   beads   ribbons
bucket   basket

Point out the ear sound (as in fear) as you read

I don't want to stay here.

As the carriage disappeared, Cinderella felt tears come to her eyes.

The palace was so near, but Cinderella feared she would never see inside it.

Sound out these words with the **ear** sound.

year   clear   beard

cheer   steer   deer

Suddenly, an old woman with glittery wings and a wand appeared!

"I'm your fairy godmother!" she said with a wave of her wand. "You will have your wish and go to the ball!"

Emphasize the w sound (as in wand)

"First, we will need to find some things," she said, with a wink.

Use your stickers to **spell** some words beginning with w.

week   wash   wool   winter

Focus on the **ng** sound (as in wi**ng**) as you read

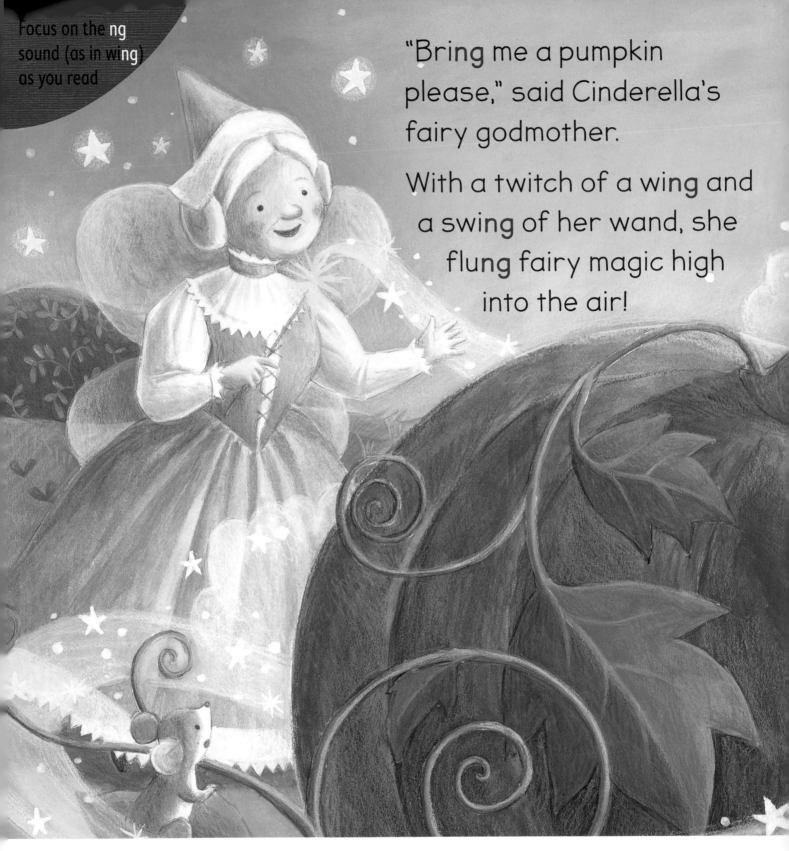

"Bring me a pumpkin please," said Cinderella's fairy godmother.

With a twitch of a wing and a swing of her wand, she flung fairy magic high into the air!

Use your stickers to **spell** some words with the **ng** sound.

king   thing   young   along

A big, ripe pumpkin from the vegetable patch grew so big it looked as if it was ready to pop!

Sound out these words with the p sound in different positions.

park   poster   paper   puppy
chip   sheep   cheap

9

Draw attention to the or sound (as in horse)

The enormous pumpkin transformed into a beautiful carriage, while four mice became stunning white horses!

Sound out these words with the or sound.

fork   corn   born   sport

short   pour   your

Emphasize the a sound (as in magic)

As the magic swirled around, a brown rat turned into a coachman and Cinderella clapped her hands.

Use your stickers to **spell** some words, which all use the a sound.

map   flag   ant   add   apple

With a clap of her hands, Cinderella's clever fairy godmother turned Cinderella's plain clothes into a glamorous gown.

Cinderella's hair became glossy, and on her feet were glittery glass slippers.

Sound out these words beginning with the cl and gl blends.

cloud   click   class   club

glove   glad   glue

12

Cinderella glowed with happiness.

"Keep a close eye on the clock," warned the fairy godmother. "The spell will end when the clock strikes twelve."

Use your stickers to **spell** some more words beginning with the cl and gl blends.

climb   cliff   glow   glare

13

Emphasize the air sound (as in hair)

As Cinderella arrived at the palace, wearing her stunning gown and with jewels in her hair, everyone turned to stare. "Who is that fair lady?" asked the prince.

Cinderella's stepsisters didn't recognize her, but they glared as she walked down the stairs.

Use your stickers to **spell** some words with the **air** sound.

there   chair   bear   share

The prince spun Cinderella into the middle of the room.

They danced all night by the light of the moon.

The prince felt he had found his true love.

Sound out these words with the oo sound.

spoon   zoo   blue   glue
chew   threw

15

Highlight
the ie sound
(as in tie)

While the dancing carried on into the night, the clock struck twelve.

Cinderella gave a frightened cry – she hadn't noticed the time!"

Stick on the speech bubbles with the ie sound.

As she ran down the flight of steps she left behind a glass slipper.

Sound out some words with the **ie** sound.

mine   smile   wild   find

tie   pie   try   by   might

Cinderella jumped into the carriage, but the magic wore off just as she started the journey home.

The carriage turned back into a giant pumpkin, the horses became mice and her gown and jewels vanished.

Use your stickers to **spell** some words with the j sound.

jug   jelly   gentle   giraffe

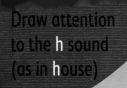

The handsome prince's heart was heavy. He had fallen in love with Cinderella, and wanted to visit every house in his country with her glass slipper.

Say the words as you spot things with the h sound.

Stick on their stickers.

18

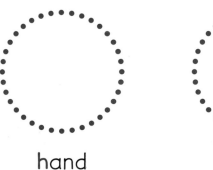 hand

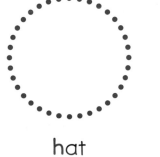 hat

 hair

"I will hunt high and low," said the prince. "Whoever this slipper fits shall be my bride."

Soon he arrived at Cinderella's home.

Sound out these words with the h sound.

hill   help   hold   hurry

whose   whole

The prince **c**alled everyone in to try on the slipper. Of **c**ourse, the stepsisters' feet **c**ouldn't fit.

Cinderella stood quietly in the **c**orner. "**C**an you try it too?" asked the prince.

Say the words as you spot things with the **k** sound.

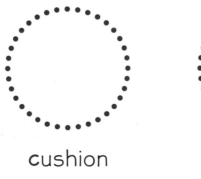 **Stick on** their stickers.

2°

cushion   cat   candle

"She can't try it on, she works in the kitchen," replied Cinderella's cunning stepmother.

The kind prince lifted Cinderella's foot onto the cushion. The slipper fitted! No one could believe it.

Use your stickers to **complete** the sentence with the k sound.

"She can't try it on, she works in the kitchen."

"I've found you!" said the kind prince. He took Cinderella's hand in his, and asked her to marry him.

Her stepsisters could only stand by and watch as the prince and Cinderella became husband and wife.

Use your stickers to **spell** some words ending with the **nd** blend.

send   band   mind   pond

22

Ask your child to **retell** the story using
these key sounds and story images.

Cinderella

bossy

wish

horses

stare

room

cry

hunt

husband

Use your stickers to **add** a word that matches
the red highlighted **sounds** on each line.

set   city   saucer   [   ]

cheer   beard   deer

bring   young   along

pumpkin   chip   pop

map   hand   add

cloud   click   clock

glad   glove   glossy

jug   gentle   giraffe

cat   kitchen   candle

24   You've had fun with phonics! Well done.